Anatomy of a Client

Negotiating with Your REAL Self

Kathryn Pape

Balboa Press books may be ordered through booksellers or by contacting:

Balboa Press
A Division of Hay House
1663 Liberty Drive
Bloomington, IN 47403
www.balboapress.com
1 (877) 407-4847

Illustrations/Photo Edits by Amy R. Womer

ISBN: 978-1-9822-4291-6 (sc)
ISBN: 978-1-9822-4292-3 (e)

Library of Congress Control Number: 2020902845

Print information available on the last page.

Balboa Press rev. date: 02/13/2020

BALBOA.PRESS
A DIVISION OF HAY HOUSE

Contents

~ DEDICATION ~

This book is dedicated To Truth-Seekers who are grateful for the 3rd Dimension "duality" experiences and are ready to move into the 4th and 5th Mind State Dimensions.

We made it be this way, so we could learn and "expand."
Lovingly forgive yourself and move on. A great new life experiencing waits.

~ACKNOWLEDGMENT~

To my family, close and far away, to my sons, daughters, grandsons and granddaughters, may you enjoy more, this changing time as we prepare for the 5th Dimension- Ascension.

Be creative and allow yourselves plenty of self-made happiness-step 1. and then share often as step 2.

~FOREWORD ~

This is my third book and each book had suffering attached. This is necessary as I had to experience the pain and struggle to get the "message."

This adventure was the most physically painful as I was learning what costly physical consequences come from unknowingly misusing my physical body. I held a deep seated false belief which resulted in pain resembling deep inward sunburn, stinging and "on fire" all over my body.

I had forgotten to realize who I was, a Biofield, and I was unknowingly into negative/against thoughts creating wildly discomforting signal intensity. My real self was signaling day and night increasing the signals as the year passed.

The client is me. The client is you. The c.l.i.e.n.t. is a customer learning intelligent and effective negotiating techniques.

The message? It is in "Anatomy of a Client."

Enjoy

~Notes~

~Notes~

Who am I?

Chapter One

Who am I?

Y ou are housed in an Electric body made of billions of moving cells. These cells in motion are moving at a given speed and give off an energy that can be detected as a *biofield*. This biofield is just a few inches away from your visible physical body and traces your body shape. This biofield can expand many feet away from your visible body. This biofield when flowing freely accounts for the presence of "happy, good and joyful" feeling sensations. This biofield when not flowing freely accounts for the presence of "uncomfortable, heavy, painful" feeling sensations.

Quantum Physics focuses on biofields finding there is a biofield present around all physical visible forms. This biofield is *atomic* in nature and flows in and out of other biofields. This atomic universe revolves around all living and is sometimes known as an *aura*.

Our human biofield/aura is in constant motion and is changeable. The speed can be increased or decreased.

The speed determines the condition of the visible physical *electric* body. The aura's speed controls the healthy appearance of the visible, physical, *electric* body.

Increasing the biofield/aura speed results in free moving energy which produces "positive, happy and glad to be alive" feeling sensations.

These sensations are the embodiment of the real *you*.

Your *electric body* is just a stage of development for you to experience the physical. As mentioned before all visible physical forms have a biofield which interacts with your *electric* body. How your invisible biofield interacts with these other biofields brings in a new cause and effect principle, an *energy cause and effect*.

CAUSE and EFFECT ENERGY

Chapter Two

CAUSE and EFFECT ENERGY

Cause is seen as starting an event and yet we now know there is a biofield to recognize. This biofield is *true* cause. The biofield's speed is creating the true *cause. Cause* is invisible to the human eye.

The only clue to the speed of a biofield is to see the physical manifested *effect*. The physical effect is visible to the human eye. The biofield holds the key to correcting or balancing the visible, physical body. Repeat! The invisible biofield is what is addressed first and then the physical visible, Electric body.

Physical visible conditions of all degrees are resulting from a proper or improper speed of the biofield. Once the speed of the biofield is increased the physical effect or visible condition will alter and disappear. A healthy appearance is the result. Your *electric* body charges or discharges from this energy cause.

The speed of the biofield is increased when this energy is unobstructed. Obstructions come from a lack of awareness that the biofield is you. As you "think," "speak," or "feel," meaning your physical sensations, your *electric* body charges or discharges. The more aware that you are your biofield the easier it is to monitor your *feelings* to determine the proper speed.

Feelings identified as *positive* such as "happy," "calm," "humorous," and "joy" are authentic signs of the proper speed. Remarkably even "sadness" and "crying" are among the positive *releasing* feelings.

Negative *feeling* sensations such as "anger" or "hate" come from your thoughts of "dislike," "disapproval," or "against." These thoughts slow the speed of the biofield to a *damaging* level which soon manifests in your physical *electric* body as an unhealthy condition.

The opposite is true of your positive *feelings* which come from thoughts such as "liking," "approval," "being for," "praising" and most of all "gratitude." These thoughts maintain the proper speed to manifest your very healthy physical *electric* body.

Your biofield consists of "color waves" or "frequencies."
This allows you to consider a *color causation* which is visible. This brings you to the new science of Inner Chromotology.

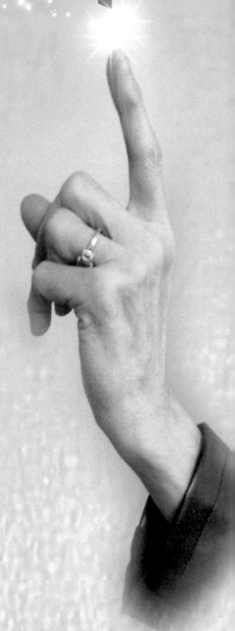

ENERGY/COLOR

Chapter Three

ENERGY/COLOR

Color is the bridge between the invisibility of the biofield and the visibility of the physical *electric* body. Seeing colors especially your "favorite" colors moves the biofield at the proper speed. The colors known as your "favorites" are special to your *electric* body, similar to a gift.

Color energy is a special category considering all the areas of involvement such as "food," "drink," "clothing," and even "thoughts." Yes, when you imagine or visualize an object with color, you evoke "color energy."

Let's talk about "color thoughts." Inner Chromotology is the study of movement of your *inner colors* through your living tissue. When you bring to mind a specific color hue, you are conversing with your *inner colors*. Your hue or shade is the proper one for the color palette of your manifested physical *electric* body. You often refer to your color palette as "warm" or "cool."

Another energy that has a match to your color energy is the energy of "sound" or "tone."

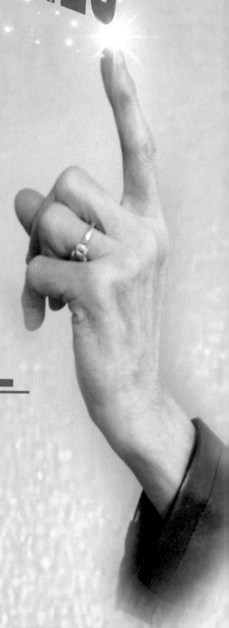

ENERGY- MUSICAL TONES

Chapter 4

ENERGY- MUSICAL TONES

Every color has a match "sound" or "tone." Your physical *electric* body has color energy centers known as "chakras." Each chakra carries a musical tone to charge the cells within your physical *electric* body.

Example: The first chakra is your "root" located at the tip of your spine. This chakra is now carrying "red –orange" coloring. The match tone is a "G" above middle "C." The speed is 792hz.

You have 6 in- the- body chakras. So you have 6 musical tones. These 6 tones match an ancient musical scale known as "Solfeggio" Scale. This scale is as follows: "G," "G#," "C," "D#," "F#," "G#."

Your matching centers and their colors are as follows: Spine- "Red-Orange"
Abdominal Cavity- "Golden –Orange"
Digestive System- "Chartreuse"
Heart- "Turquoise"
Throat- "Blue/Aqua"(cool/warm pallet)
Brow- "Blue Violet"/"Red Violet"(cool/warm pallet)

You can keep your biofield at the proper speed by toning, singing or being "tuned" with Angelic Tuning Forks. Solfeggio CDS are available for your listening. You give yourself a "gift" when you recharge/ rebalance through the Solfeggio "tones" and imagine the match "colors."

Recall the message shared in Chapter Two- "Obstructions come from a lack of awareness of you as a biofield while you "think." Thinking thoughts, color or not, leads us into the reason or motive for the thought. This is called "intention."

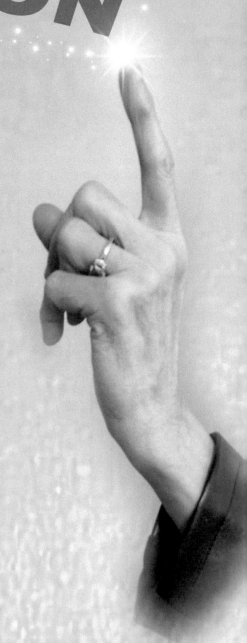

INTENTION

Chapter Five

<u>INTENTION</u>

Y ou will not automatically focus on the *intention* of your thoughts without realizing that you are a biofield housed in an electric body. Concerning you, a biofield, there is one important intention- to keep the *speed* of the biofield *at its proper movement*. This proper movement *is* the only way you can be happy. Happiness and health are reflections of each other.

Study the effects of positive *feeling so good* sensations and compare them to negative uncontrolled *feeling* sensations and you alone are deciding what you want to experience. Is it happiness or misery?

As both are self-made sensations you decide, according to how you see yourself: Victim or Director, not deserving or deserving.

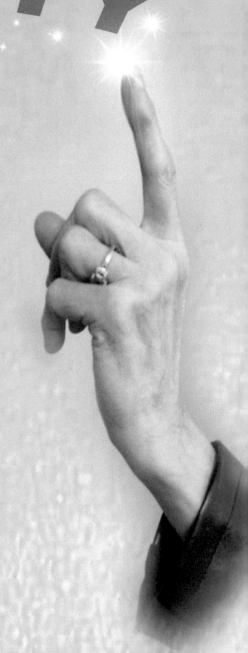

CLARITY

Chapter Six

CLARITY

Being clear about what you want is *you* directing your life. Victims do not take control of their lives for happy outcomes. You as a director of your life can have as much control of your life as you desire. This is why it is so important to realize and protect your "real self," your biofield.

Your biofield maintains the proper speed when you are positive. When you are clear about what you want, the thoughts on *seeing/imaging yourself* with it causes the field to speed up. This creates your strong *feeling of desire.* This clear genuine desire is energy that serves as a *magnet* pulling the dream toward you and charges the *electric* body.

When you become *doubtful*, or worse *ungrateful* and *impatient*, the biofield slows down, discharging and you are left with self- made disappointing, frustrating, and slightly angry feeling sensations to experience. *Gratitude*, a great attitude, is the key.

The biofield exists on *thought*, *color* and *sound frequencies*.
You create an *invisible force* that *magnetically* pulls the dream closer when you express gratitude by thought, spoken or not, as if you already possess your dream.

Thinking or talking about the details, seeing color, hearing sounds, if appropriate, and most of all *feeling strong genuine desire* are the steps necessary for the magic of *you* to co-create your dream.

Trust! This is the big challenge. The energies of genuine trust, feeling that all is ok, you are deserving, and your intention is honorable push the dream into reality.

Not being clear about what you want will bring confusion and parts of a dream, now a nightmare. Your "dream" takes so long you begin to build fear or doubt that you can manifest your dreams.

The *Law of attraction* works all the time. It is law and must bring you what you subconsciously request consciously- Creator or Victim. This is why *trust* is very important.

BELIEF SYSTEM-Director or VICTIM

Chapter 7

BELIEF SYSTEM-
Director or VICTIM

A belief system is a *series of ideas* or *values* you set or adopted around a specific topic such as food, medicine, people, religion, fashion or even social customs. The beliefs start quite young, are grouped and recorded through learning. This learning can be by experience (participant) or recorded (spectator).

Why is this important? All value setting is a part of belief systems. The more closed minded, *"sure it is this way, only,"* the more rigid the belief system you hold. This restricts your field. Remember the value starts as an *idea*.

Your *chosen values* determine your actions. Believing that you are a victim, you choose to see outside circumstances more important than yourself. Your conscious or unconscious *plan* of action will be against your dream. In fact, seeing yourself as a victim there usually is not a "dream." Victims value ideas that cancel out the truth of what they really are: directors.

Directing your life is deciding the steps you want to happen, visualizing and "feeling" the confidence energy that you, a biofield, send out through you. Here you are developing your ideas *respecting your energy* and that of others. *Guidance* inside is your heritage from being in tune with your biofield-you. That "happy feeling" is the result of being in tune.

The biofield awaits direction or directs itself by laws you are learning about here. Realizing you *are* the biofield and that proper speed of the movements are the important values to consider, your choice of thought, positive thought about *yourself* and your *surroundings* set the *Law of Attraction* action in your favor.

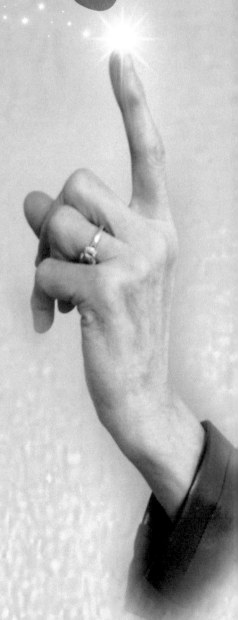

THOUGHTS

Chapter 8

THOUGHTS

Thoughts, spoken or not, are *vibrations* which pass through the biofield into the physical *electric* body. Thoughts charge or discharge your *electric* body. Realizing you *are* a biofield appearing physical in an *electric* body, you begin to monitor your *feelings* which are directly connected to your thoughts.

Yes, you are *feeling* your thoughts. Happy, pleasurable and secure feelings are only possible when you are thinking thoughts that praise, appreciate and shower love *on you*. That is right.

Your biofield, the *real* you, is moving other vibrations through you in the form of color, material, and sound *for your enjoyment*. Higher faster moving vibrations are energy matches to you such as *favorites*.

Thoughts which become judgmental or critical of *you* slow your biofield and begin to show unhealthy conditions in your physical *electric* body. Thoughts critical of others will register as thoughts *against* you as your biofield, the real you, recognizes thought vibration and passes it through you. You are experiencing what it is to be *connected to all other vibrations* and *biofields*.

Positive thought protects the moment as "it is" so you can see that it is *neutral*. It is acting like a mirror. You experience the "good," "enjoyable" and "happy" *feelings* as proof of your trust in you. Your biofield, the *real* you, is charging the *electric* body, raising the voltage it needs.

Negative thought is the opposite. *Any critical or judgmental* thought changes the biofield's speed and soon discharges lowering the voltage the *electric* body needs. On a molecular level the *atoms group and then attack inside the vibrations of sound and "tones."* (Reference Chapter 4)

Negative thought changes the *outcome* of the situation that is being built and drawn to you by the *Law of Attraction*. It works *against* the truth of what you *can* experience. So much *needless suffering* and *trouble*, save a lesson to learn quickly, are the results of you thinking negatively. Conditions appearing in the physical *electric* body which are simple allergies or dis-easing start with the "against" thought. Here is the purpose of you forgiving you.

You will forgive you once you understand the truth that *you are a biofield* housed in an *electric* body as are all others, and the *power of your attitude*.

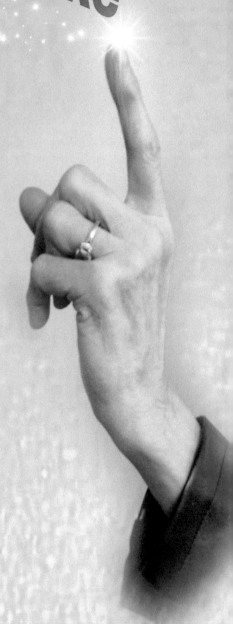

ATTITUDE- Like/not Like

Chapter 9

ATTITUDE- Like/not Like

You know this word *attitude*. You have judged someone speaking about something as having a positive attitude or negative attitude. A *negative* attitude impression follows complaints and frequent arguments. Whereas a *positive* attitude follows one who agrees and finds *delight* in most circumstances. The common denominator for a positive attitude is *liking the happening*.

In energy the *liking thought* is a vibration which passes through the biofield into the *electric* body causing an increase, a charging, a *lifting*, in the speed resulting in a "happy" feeling. The more *liking thoughts* you make, the faster the biofield moves, charging the electric body resulting in higher happier sensations. These sensations are magical to you, appearance wise, and result in benefiting all others in unseen ways.

The opposite occurs in the *not liking* thought. The vibration causes your biofield, the real you, to lower the speed and discharge resulting in lowered voltage. When you think or choose to "dislike," the vibration passes through into the physical *electric* body as "uncomfortable," "irritating," and "painful." Finally, death on a molecular level begins to happen and has to be felt, physically.

How serious the resulting condition is, depends on the intention, strong belief and continuous negative thinking. Anger into Hate *"against"* thoughts yield the "discomforting," "out of control" and "ready to explode" *feeling* sensations. These negative feelings often lead you to irrational behavior.

This of course causes the *Law of Attraction* to bring trouble and suffering to you, first, then spreads outward affecting others.

Tip: choosing "to like," and "to love" thoughts is to order your biofield to *increase* in speed and you experience natural "delightful," and "most happy" *feelings* referred to as "joy."

Thoughts are established through the years through "words." Let's take a look at *word vibrations* and your biofield.

WORDS

Chapter 10

<u>**WORDS**</u>

Regardless of language *Words*, thoughts, spoken or not, are vibrations you *feel* as you think. The vibrations pass through your biofield and subtly affect your physical electric body. Every word has a definition which passes through your biofield.

If that definition's meaning implies an *against* concept or *negative separation*, the energy *slows, discharges and lowers the voltage the electric body needs.* The energy can move in an opposite direction, causing a serious obstruction. Subtly, you have commanded your physical *electric* body to go *against itself* or separate from the life force biofield. This is known as dis- easing.

Alas, you start to learn definitions very early from parenting and schools. Every day you are exposed to a new word, whether slang or a power controlling jargon.

Until now you may have not understood the energy biofields involved. Neither do the modern dictionaries understand human energy laws. Keep reading and you will see a few new definitions which *direct* the *vibration correctly.*

DEFINITIONS- pro/con: for/against

Chapter 11

DEFINITIONS- pro/con: for/against

A definition explains the meaning of a word usually decided by a committee innocently ignorant of energy vibration. Now that you are learning about *human energy, biofields* and *your electric body* you can take more control.

You are here to discover how to *run vibrations through your* bio*field*, charging your electric body to create *feelings* of *joy*. You are free to create any definition that feels *good* thinking of it. It is your happiness and health that matter.

You already direct your energy from an idea in a definition. Now check to see how it *feels* as that vibration does one of two things- nurtures your energy (increases speed/charges) or negates (depletes your energy speed/discharges).

You can monitor your *feelings* to see the common denominator of good and happy feelings is a *pro* or *for* definition. Also monitoring your angry, disappointed, worry or frustrated *feelings* shows a common denominator as *against* or *con* definition.

You can change the definition of a word to raise the vibration level. This requires you to be willing to create a *new perspective* of the word. An approach you can use to address your biofield, the opposite of your physical *electric* body, is known as an *acronym*.

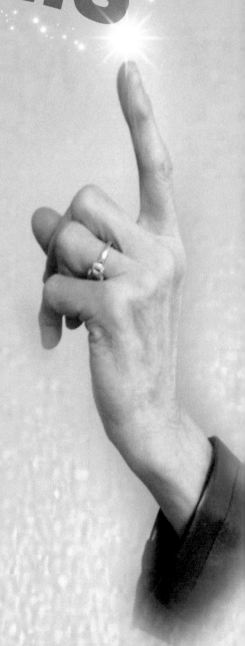

ACRONYMS

Chapter 12

ACRONYMS

As all vibrations are rising so must *word* vibrations. An acronym is a new *word meaning* made from the letters of the word such as "acronym"- (an) *approach clearly revealing* (the) *opposite nature, yes,* (of) *mankind.* (Some smoother reading words are in parenthesis.) Please, note the principle.

Acronyms bring measurably higher frequencies of the former definition. A scientific principle is found in many acronyms involved in human energy. This explains the *benefit* or *harm* of the *definition idea.*

Another example is the word *against.* You understand this word to mean *opposing* or *non- uniting.* Yet what is now understood is this word or thought commands your *atoms* (to) *group* (and) *attack inside, natural sounds* (and) *tones.* (Reference Kathryn's book *Harmonious Communication With Yourself.*)

Another example is the word *like.* Every time you *decide* you like you, someone, something, or some place, you feel a good *feeling.* This is because the word *like* bonds the vibrations.

The acronym for *like* is *lift individual kinetic energy.* You are kinetic and potential energies. The command is to *lift* or *speed up* the individual's energy field. This is why *"I like"* or *"I love"* words or thoughts *feel* so good.

Now look at *dislike.* This word feels strong when building anger, yet, *dislike* is a *negative separating* vibration.

When you choose to "dislike," you are *developing ideas* (which) *stop/slow* (the) *lifting* (of) *individual kinetic energy.*

Another example is the word *feel.* You understand this as a physical touch or inner sensation. When you feel, you are forming energy as you pass this word through you that is essential to life, to learn or love. So the acronym is *forming energy essential* (to) *live/learn/love.* All are true.

Another example is a word you innocently use to harm you and others: *offend.* You see this as something you want to avoid or decide to be against, to dislike.

Since *you* are making your *feelings* through passing thoughts/words through you, a biofield, the object, issue or person you credit as offending you is *neutral.* You are choosing to dislike, slowing the field and feeling the discomfort.

So, a clearer definition that reveals what is happening is *openly forming* (a) *false expression* (usually talk) *nurturing damage*-you, cellular-wise, others, example.

As you learn about your *self-made feelings* you are to think for yourself, love yourself, and learn new ways to hear and speak that keep your biofield at proper speed.

You are a beautiful perfect soul. Understand, *soul* as a *substance on* (a) *universal level*. Yes, *energy* is the universal substance. You are a vibrational energy biofield. *Perfect* is better seen as a *perfecting journey* that is endless as is energy.

Now you have the steps for negotiating with yourself.
Enjoy yourself in the physical world having a physical *electric* body you can control by making *positive thoughts into feelings* out of your energy biofield.

Love and Light,

Kathryn- watch for my new dictionary-

P.A.P.E. Directionary and enjoy "Oh My Word!"

Author's Biography

Ever wonder who you really are? Anatomy of a Client focuses on identifying your REAL self as a Biofield housed in an Electric body. Anatomy explains how to live with this Electric body.

Kathryn Pape is a Sound and Color practitioner using Angelic Tuning Forks and the Solfeggio scale to balance the clients' chakras which greatly affects the Biofield. Kathryn has spent 30+ years as a cognitive curriculum specialist.

Kathryn founded the field known as "Human Energy Conservation"- understood as better use of me by me.

Other publications are "Always Like the First Time" and "Harmonious Communication With Yourself."

Facebook:
www.facebook.com/papecreativeeducationservices.com

Website: www.papecreativeeducationservices.com

Printed in the United States
By Bookmasters